150 Life Quotes Inspiring the Happy, Good and Funny in Life

Phil Collins

Dedication

To the seekers of joy, the believers in laughter, and the embracers of life's myriad hues, this book is dedicated. May these life-affirming quotes serve as guiding stars, igniting happiness, goodness, and humor in every moment.

Here's to celebrating life's tapestry and finding inspiration in its most delightful and profound moments.

Table of Contents

Introduction

Welcome to a collection of 150 life-affirming quotes that celebrate the beauty, joy, and humor woven into the fabric of our existence.

Through these inspiring words, discover the essence of happiness, goodness, and the delightful quirks that make life an extraordinary journey.

Let these quotes be your daily companion, guiding you towards a brighter, more fulfilling life.

150 Life Quotes

Inspiring the Happy, Good and Funny in Life

1. "The purpose of our lives is to be happy."
    — Dalai Lama

2. "Life is what happens when you're busy
making other plans."
    — John Lennon

3. "Get busy living or get busy dying."
— **Stephen King**

4. "You only live once, but if you do it right,
once is enough."
— **Mae West**

5. "Many of life's failures are people who did
not realize how close they were to success
when they gave up."
– Thomas A. Edison

6. "If you want to live a happy life, tie it to a
goal, not to people or things."
– Albert Einstein

7. "Never let the fear of striking out keep you
from playing the game."
– Babe Ruth

8. "Money and success don't change people;
they merely amplify what is already there."
— Will Smith

9. "Your time is limited, so don't waste it living someone else's life. Don't be trapped by dogma – which is living with the results of other people's thinking."
– Steve Jobs

10. "Not how long, but how well you have lived is the main thing."
— Seneca

11. "If life were predictable it would cease to
be life, and be without flavor."
– Eleanor Roosevelt

12. "The whole secret of a successful life is to
find out what is one's destiny to do, and
then do it."
– Henry Ford

13. "In order to write about life first you must live it."
– Ernest Hemingway

14. "The big lesson in life, baby, is never be scared of anyone or anything."
– Frank Sinatra

15. "Sing like no one's listening, love like you've never been hurt, dance like nobody's watching, and live like it's heaven on earth."
– Anonymous

16. "Curiosity about life in all of its aspects, I think, is still the secret of great creative people."
– Leo Burnett

17. "Life is not a problem to be solved, but a
reality to be experienced."
– Soren Kierkegaard

18. "The unexamined life is not worth
living."
— Socrates

19. "Turn your wounds into wisdom."
— Oprah Winfrey

20. "The way I see it, if you want the
rainbow, you gotta put up with the rain."
— Dolly Parton

21. "Do all the good you can, for all the people you can, in all the ways you can, as long as you can." — **Hillary Clinton**

22. "Don't settle for what life gives you; make life better and build something."
— **Ashton Kutcher**

23. "Everybody wants to be famous, but nobody wants to do the work. I live by that. You grind hard so you can play hard. At the end of the day, you put all the work in, and eventually it'll pay off. It could be in a year, it could be in 30 years. Eventually, your hard work will pay off."
— **Kevin Hart**

24. "Everything negative – pressure, challenges – is all an opportunity for me to rise."
— **Kobe Bryant**

25. "I like criticism. It makes you strong."
— **LeBron James**

26. "You never really learn much from
hearing yourself speak."
— **George Clooney**

27. "Life imposes things on you that you can't control, but you still have the choice of how you're going to live through this."
— **Celine Dion**

28. "Life is never easy. There is work to be done and obligations to be met – obligations to truth, to justice, and to liberty."
— **John F. Kennedy**

29. "Live for each second without hesitation."
— **Elton John**

30. "Life is like riding a bicycle. To keep your balance, you must keep moving."
— **Albert Einstein**

31. "Life is really simple, but men insist on
making it complicated."
— **Confucius**

32. "Life is a succession of lessons which
must be lived to be understood."
— **Helen Keller**

33. "Your work is going to fill a large part of your life, and the only way to be truly satisfied is to do what you believe is great work. And the only way to do great work is to love what you do. If you haven't found it yet, keep looking. Don't settle. As with all matters of the heart, you'll know when you find it."
— **Steve Jobs**

34. "My mama always said, life is like a box of chocolates. You never know what you're gonna get."
— **Forrest Gump**

35. "Watch your thoughts; they become
words. Watch your words; they become
actions. Watch your actions; they become
habits. Watch your habits; they become
character. Watch your character; it becomes
your destiny."
— **Lao-Tze**

36. "When we do the best we can, we never
know what miracle is wrought in our life or
the life of another."
— **Helen Keller**

37. "The healthiest response to life is joy."
— **Deepak Chopra**

38. "Life is like a coin. You can spend it any way you wish, but you only spend it once."
— **Lillian Dickson**

39. "The best portion of a good man's life is his little nameless, unencumbered acts of kindness and of love."
— **Wordsworth**

40. "In three words I can sum up everything I've learned about life: It goes on."
— **Robert Frost**

41. "Life is ten percent what happens to you and ninety percent how you respond to it."
— Charles Swindoll

42. "Keep calm and carry on."
— Winston Churchill

43. "Maybe that's what life is... a wink of the
eye and winking stars."
— Jack Kerouac

44. "Life is a flower of which love is the
honey."
— Victor Hugo

45. "Keep smiling, because life is a beautiful thing and there's so much to smile about." — **Marilyn Monroe**

46. "Health is the greatest gift, contentment the greatest wealth, faithfulness the best relationship." — **Buddha**

47. "You have brains in your head. You have feet in your shoes. You can steer yourself in any direction you choose."
— **Dr. Seuss**

48. "Good friends, good books, and a sleepy conscience: this is the ideal life."
— **Mark Twain**

49. "Life would be tragic if it weren't funny."
— **Stephen Hawking**

50. "Live in the sunshine, swim in the sea,
drink the wild air."
— **Ralph Waldo Emerson**

51. "The greatest pleasure of life is love."
— **Euripides**

52. "Life is what we make it, always has been, always will be."
— **Grandma Moses**

53. "Life's tragedy is that we get old too soon
and wise too late."
— **Benjamin Franklin**

54. "Life is about making an impact, not
making an income."
— **Kevin Kruse**

55. "I've missed more than 9000 shots in my career. I've lost almost 300 games. 26 times I've been trusted to take the game winning shot and missed. I've failed over and over and over again in my life. And that is why I succeed."
— **Michael Jordan**

56. "Every strike brings me closer to the next home run."
— **Babe Ruth**

57. "The two most important days in your life are the day you are born and the day you find out why. – **Mark Twain**

58. "Life shrinks or expands in proportion to one's courage."
– **Anais Nin**

59. "When I was 5 years old, my mother always told me that happiness was the key to life. When I went to school, they asked me what I wanted to be when I grew up. I wrote down 'happy'. They told me I didn't understand the assignment, and I told them they didn't understand life."
– John Lennon

60. "Too many of us are not living our dreams because we are living our fears."
– Les Brown

61. "I believe every human has a finite number of heartbeats. I don't intend to waste any of mine."
— **Neil Armstrong**

62. "Live as if you were to die tomorrow. Learn as if you were to live forever."
— **Mahatma Gandhi**

63. "If you live long enough, you'll make mistakes. But if you learn from them, you'll be a better person."
— **Bill Clinton**

64. "Life is short, and it is here to be lived."
— **Kate Winslet**

65. "The longer I live, the more beautiful life becomes."
— Frank Lloyd Wright

66. "Every moment is a fresh beginning."
— T.S. Eliot

67. "When you cease to dream you cease to live." — **Malcolm Forbes**

68. "If you spend your whole life waiting for the storm, you'll never enjoy the sunshine." — **Morris West**

69. "Don't cry because it's over, smile because it happened."
— **Dr. Seuss**

70. "If you can do what you do best and be happy, you're further along in life than most people."
— **Leonardo DiCaprio**

71. "We should remember that just as a positive outlook on life can promote good health, so can everyday acts of kindness."
— **Hillary Clinton**

72. "Don't limit yourself. Many people limit themselves to what they think they can do. You can go as far as your mind lets you. What you believe, remember, you can achieve."
— **Mary Kay Ash**

73. "It is our choices that show what we truly are, far more than our abilities."
— **J. K. Rowling**

74. "If you're not stubborn, you'll give up on experiments too soon. And if you're not flexible, you'll pound your head against the wall and you won't see a different solution to a problem you're trying to solve."
— **Jeff Bezos**

75. "The best way to predict your future is to create it."
— **Abraham Lincoln**

76. "You must expect great things from yourself before you can do them."
— **Michael Jordan**

77. "Identity is a prison you can never escape, but the way to redeem your past is not to run from it, but to try to understand it, and use it as a foundation to grow."
— **Jay-Z**

78. "There are no mistakes, only opportunities."
— **Tina Fey**

79. "It takes 20 years to build a reputation and five minutes to ruin it. If you think about that, you'll do things differently."
— **Warren Buffett**

80. "As you grow older, you will discover that you have two hands, one for helping yourself, the other for helping others."
— **Audrey Hepburn**

81. "Sometimes you can't see yourself clearly until you see yourself through the eyes of others."
— **Ellen DeGeneres**

82. "You must not lose faith in humanity. Humanity is an ocean; if a few drops of the ocean are dirty, the ocean does not become dirty."
— **Mahatma Gandhi**

83. "All life is an experiment. The more experiments you make, the better."
– Ralph Waldo Emerson

84. "Here's to the crazy ones, the misfits, the rebels, the troublemakers, the round pegs in the square holes … the ones who see things differently — they're not fond of rules … You can quote them, disagree with them, glorify or vilify them, but the only thing you can't do is ignore them because they change things … They push the human race forward, and while some may see them as the crazy ones, we see genius …"
– Steve Jobs

85. "It had long come to my attention that people of accomplishment rarely sat back and let things happen to them. They went out and things happened."
— **Leonardo Da Vinci**

86. "Throughout life people will make you mad, disrespect you and treat you bad. Let God deal with the things they do, cause hate in your heart will consume you too."
— **Will Smith**

87. "Do not dwell in the past, do not dream of the future, concentrate the mind on the present moment."
– **Buddha**

88. "Life is a dream for the wise, a game for the fool, a comedy for the rich, a tragedy for the poor." – **Sholom Aleichem**

89. "If you love life, don't waste time, for
time is what life is made up of."
– Bruce Lee

90. When one door closes, another opens;
but we often look so long and so regretfully
upon the closed door that we do not see the
one that has opened for us.
– Alexander Graham Bell

91. "Never take life seriously. Nobody gets
out alive anyway."
— **Anonymous**

92. "Be happy for this moment. This
moment is your life."
– **Omar Khayyam**

93. "Happiness is the feeling that power
increases — that resistance is being
overcome."
— Friedrich Nietzsche

94. "I have learned to seek my happiness by
limiting my desires, rather than in
attempting to satisfy them."
— John Stuart Mill

95. "The secret of happiness, you see, is not found in seeking more, but in developing the capacity to enjoy less."
- Socrates

96. "The more man meditates upon good thoughts, the better will be his world and the world at large."
— Confucius

97. "The greatest blessings of mankind are within us and within our reach. A wise man is content with his lot, whatever it may be, without wishing for what he has not."
— **Seneca**

98. "Happiness is like a butterfly; the more you chase it, the more it will elude you, but if you turn your attention to other things, it will come and sit softly on your shoulder."
— **Henry David Thoreau**

99. "When it is obvious that goals can't be reached, don't adjust the goals, but adjust the action steps."
— **Confucius**

100. "There may be people who have more talent than you, but there's no excuse for anyone to work harder than you do – and I believe that."
— **Derek Jeter**

101. "Don't be afraid to fail. It's not the end of the world, and in many ways, it's the first step toward learning something and getting better at it."
— **Jon Hamm**

102. "Life is very interesting... in the end, some of your greatest pains become your greatest strengths."
– **Drew Barrymore**

103. "I think if you live in a black-and-white world, you're gonna suffer a lot. I used to be like that. But I don't believe that anymore."
– Bradley Cooper

104. "I don't believe in happy endings, but I do believe in happy travels, because ultimately, you die at a very young age, or you live long enough to watch your friends die. It's a mean thing, life."
– George Clooney

105. "It's never too late – never too late to start over, never too late to be happy."
– Jane Fonda

106. "You're only human. You live once and life is wonderful, so eat the damned red velvet cupcake." **– Emma Stone**

107. "A lot of people give up just before they're about to make it. You know you never know when that next obstacle is going to be the last one."
– Chuck Norris

108. "Be nice to people on the way up, because you may meet them on the way down."
– Jimmy Durante

109. "I believe you make your day. You make your life. So much of it is all perception, and this is the form that I built for myself. I have to accept it and work within those compounds, and it's up to me."
– Brad Pitt

110. "The minute that you're not learning I believe you're dead."
– Jack Nicholson

111. "Life's tough, but it's tougher when you're stupid."
— John Wayne

112. "Take up one idea. Make that one idea your life -- think of it, dream of it, live on that idea. Let the brain, muscles, nerves, every part of your body be full of that idea, and just leave every other idea alone. This is the way to success."
— Swami Vivekananda

113. "I guess it comes down to a simple choice, really. Get busy living or get busy dying."
— **Shawshank Redemption**

114. "When we strive to become better than we are, everything around us becomes better too."
— **Paulo Coelho**

115. "There are three things you can do with your life: You can waste it, you can spend it, or you can invest it. The best use of your life is to invest it in something that will last longer than your time on Earth."
— **Rick Warren**

116. "You only pass through this life once, you don't come back for an encore."
— **Elvis Presley**

117. "In the long run, the sharpest weapon of
all is a kind and gentle spirit."
— **Anne Frank**

118. "You're not defined by your past; you're
prepared by it. You're stronger, more
experienced, and you have greater
confidence."
— **Joel Osteen**

119. "We become not a melting pot but a beautiful mosaic. Different people, different beliefs, different yearnings, different hopes, different dreams."
— **Jimmy Carter**

120. "Nothing is more honorable than a grateful heart."
— **Seneca**

121. "Once you figure out who you are and what you love about yourself, I think it all kinda falls into place."
— **Jennifer Aniston**

122. "Happy is the man who can make a living by his hobby."
— **George Bernard Shaw**

123. "Just disconnect. Once in a day sometimes, sit silently and from all connections disconnect yourself."
— **Yoda**

124. "Be where you are; otherwise you will miss your life."
— **Buddha**

125. "Living an experience, a particular fate,
is accepting it fully."
— **Albert Camus**

126. "The more you praise and celebrate
your life, the more there is in life to
celebrate."
— **Oprah Winfrey**

127. "Your image isn't your character. Character is what you are as a person."
— **Derek Jeter**

128. "Football is like life, it requires perseverance, self-denial, hard work, sacrifice, dedication and respect for authority."
—**Vince Lombardi**

129. "As you know, life is an echo; we get what we give."
— **David DeNotaris**

130. "There are no regrets in life, just lessons."
— **Jennifer Aniston**

131. "I believe that nothing in life is unimportant. Every moment can be a beginning."
— **John McLeod**

132. "Find people who will make you better."
— **Michelle Obama**

133. "As my knowledge of things grew I felt more and more the delight of the world I was in."
— **Helen Keller**

134. "Benjamin Franklin was a humanitarian that dedicated his life to making contributions to all humans. He had a clear purpose for himself: improve the human race."
— **Paulo Braga**

135. "You cannot control everything that happens to you; you can only control the way you respond to what happens. Your response is your power." — **Anonymous**

136. "Don't allow your past or present condition to control you. It's just a process that you're going through to get you to the next level."
— **T.D. Jakes**

137. "You will meet two kinds of people in life: ones who build you up and ones who tear you down. But in the end, you'll thank them both."
— **Anonymous**

138. "My mission in life is not merely to survive, but to thrive; and to do so with some passion, some compassion, some humor, and some style." – **Maya Angelou**

139. "If we don't change, we don't grow. If we don't grow, we aren't really living."
— **Gail Sheehy**

140. "You choose the life you live. If you don't like it, it's on you to change it because no one else is going to do it for you."
— **Kim Kiyosaki**

141. "It is impossible to live without failing at something, unless you live so cautiously, that you might as well not have lived at all — in which case you fail by default."
— **Anonymous**

142. "Life doesn't require that we be the best, only that we try our best."
– **H. Jackson Brown Jr.**

143. "The way I see it, every life is a pile of good things and bad things. The good things don't always soften the bad things, but vice versa, the bad things don't always spoil the good things and make them unimportant."
– Doctor Who

144. "Life isn't about waiting for the storm to pass, it's about learning to dance in the rain."
– Vivian Greene

145. "I enjoy life when things are happening.
I don't care if it's good or bad. That means
you're alive."
– Joan Rivers

146. "There's more to life than basketball.
The most important thing is your family and
taking care of each other and loving each
other no matter what."
– Stephen Curry

147. "Today, you have 100% of your life left."
– Tom Landry

148. "Nobody who ever gave his best
regretted it." **– George Halas**

149. "Make each day your masterpiece."
— **John Wooden**

150. "You can't put a limit on anything. The more you dream, the farther you get."
— **Michael Phelps**

Closing Remark

May these life-affirming quotes continue to inspire laughter, happiness, and a deeper appreciation for the beautiful moments life gifts us.

As you navigate the journey of existence, may these words linger as reminders to cherish every joy, overcome every challenge, and embrace the tapestry of experiences that shape our lives.

Here's to a life filled with inspiration, joy, and an enduring sense of wonder.